whitestar kids

THIS IS A TRAVEL JOURNAL

TEXT AND ILLUSTRATIONS BY
PRISCA PRIANO

LET ME WELCOME YOU TO THIS DIARY,

_______________________________!

WRITE YOUR NAME HERE

SOMEONE TOLD ME THAT YOU ARE ABOUT
TO GO PLACES...

MAYBE YOU DIDN'T KNOW THIS, BUT SOME PANDAS
WILL COME WITH YOU ON VACATION
TO HELP YOU WRITE ABOUT YOUR JOURNEY!
SO, TO BEGIN,
DRAW AN X ON THE PLACE YOU ARE GOING.

EVERYONE KNOWS PANDAS
ARE THE SOUL OF VACATIONS.
PACK A FEW OTHER THINGS IN YOUR SUITCASE
AND TOGETHER YOU WILL ENJOY
GREAT ADVENTURES!

THIS DIARY | PENCILS AND MARKERS | GLUE | YOUR CREATIVITY!

REMEMBER THAT YOU CAN WRITE ANYTHING YOU WANT HERE, WHEN YOU WANT TO AND IN THE WAY THAT YOU WANT (YOU CAN EVEN SKIP PAGES IF YOU LIKE).
THE ONLY THING YOU HAVE TO DO ON VACATION IS HAVE FUN!

SHALL WE START?

☐ SURE!! ☐ NOT YET...

LET'S WARM UP
GO!

FIRST OF ALL:

WHAT DOES IT MEAN FOR YOU TO GO ON VACATION?

TRY TO EXPLAIN IT
BY DRAWING THE BEST MEMORY ABOUT A TRIP
THAT YOU'VE MADE ON THE LAPTOP
(OR PASTE A PHOTO!).

PANDA PC / PHOTO / MY-GREATEST-VACATION

DO YOU NEED A REMINDER? HERE ARE THE

A NORMAL DAY

DIFFERENCES BETWEEN...

AND A VACATION

WHAT IS YOUR VACATION PERSONALITY?

FIND OUT WITH THIS TEST!

YOUR IDEAL VACATION:

A) CAMPING

B) WORLD TOUR

C) AMUSEMENT PARK TOUR

D) A FAMOUS CITY

YOUR FAVORITE ANIMAL:

A) WOLF

B) KANGAROO

C) DOLPHIN

D) DOG

ON VACATION YOU LIKE T

A) LOOK OUT THE WINDOW

B) KEEP A DIARY

C) PLAY WITH POCKET GAMES

D) MAKE FRIENDS WITH OTHER TRAVELERS

THE PERFECT SOUVENIR:

A) AN INTERESTING ROCK YOU HAVE FOUND

B) A MAGNET

C) A PUZZLE OF A MONUMENT

D) A SHINY PIN

ON VACATION YOU SNACK ON:

A) FRUIT

B) THE LOCAL DELICACY

C) A TOWER OF COOKIES

D) ICE CREAM WITH FRIENDS

CHOOSE A COLOR:

A) BLUE

B) RED

C) YELLOW

D) BLACK

YOUR FAVORITE TRANSPORTATION:

A) CANOE

B) HOT AIR BALLOON

C) SCOOTER

D) SPACE ROCKET

SEE WHICH LETTER YOU CIRCLED MOST OFTEN, THEN TURN THE PAGE!

THE RESULTS!

YOUR VACATION PERSONALITY IS...

A

B

WILD

ON VACATION YOU ARE ALWAYS UP FOR SOME ADVENTUROUS EXPLORATIONS, WHETHER IT'S RAINY OR SUNNY OUTSIDE! CAVES, RIVERS, AND ROCK WALLS ARE SO IRRESISTIBLE TO YOU THAT YOU'RE NOT AFRAID OF BAND-AIDS OR BRUISES.

NOMADIC

YOUR SUITCASE ALWAYS CONTAINS SOMETHING FROM HOME: A FAMILY PHOTO, YOUR SPECIAL PILLOW, THE GOLDFISH IN YOUR FISH BOWL. BUT IT'S NOT NOSTALGIA! YOU YOU ARE ALWAYS UP FOR TRAVELING, YOU JUST BRING YOUR HOME WITH YOU.

PLAYFUL

FROM WHEN YOU WAKE UP UNTIL BEDTIME, YOU HAVE ONLY ONE THOUGHT ON YOUR MIND: PLAY MORE!

YOU WOULD PLAY SOCCER EVEN ON TOP OF KILIMANJARO, AND YOU ALWAYS CARRY A DECK OF WATERPROOF CARDS FOR A QUICK GAME ON THE PADDLE BOAT.

SPARKLING

WHEREVER YOU GO ON VACATION, YOU CERTAINLY STAND OUT!

EVERYONE COMES LOOKING FOR YOU TO GO FOR A BIKE RIDE, AND YOU'VE LOST COUNT OF THE AMOUNT OF ICE CREAM PEOPLE HAVE OFFERED YOU.

YOUR JOURNEY IS ABOUT TO START.

WRITE DOWN 3 THINGS (THAT YOU NORMALLY DO EVERY DAY) THAT YOU CAN FINALLY SKIP ON VACATION.

ON VACATION I WON'T...

1)

2)

3)

PREPARATIONS

WHAT KIND OF JOURNEY DO YOU EXPECT?

MOOD TRACKER

COME BACK HERE TO DRAW YOUR FACE

AS THE DEPARTURE DATE APPROACHES

THE IDEA OF THIS VACATION:
WAS MINE
SOMEONE ELSE'S
IT WAS A VOTE
TUMMY UP
EVERYTHING FOR YOUR RELAXATION
SPECIAL VACATION IN:
-2
-1
LET'S GO!

WHO IS TRAVELING WITH YOU?

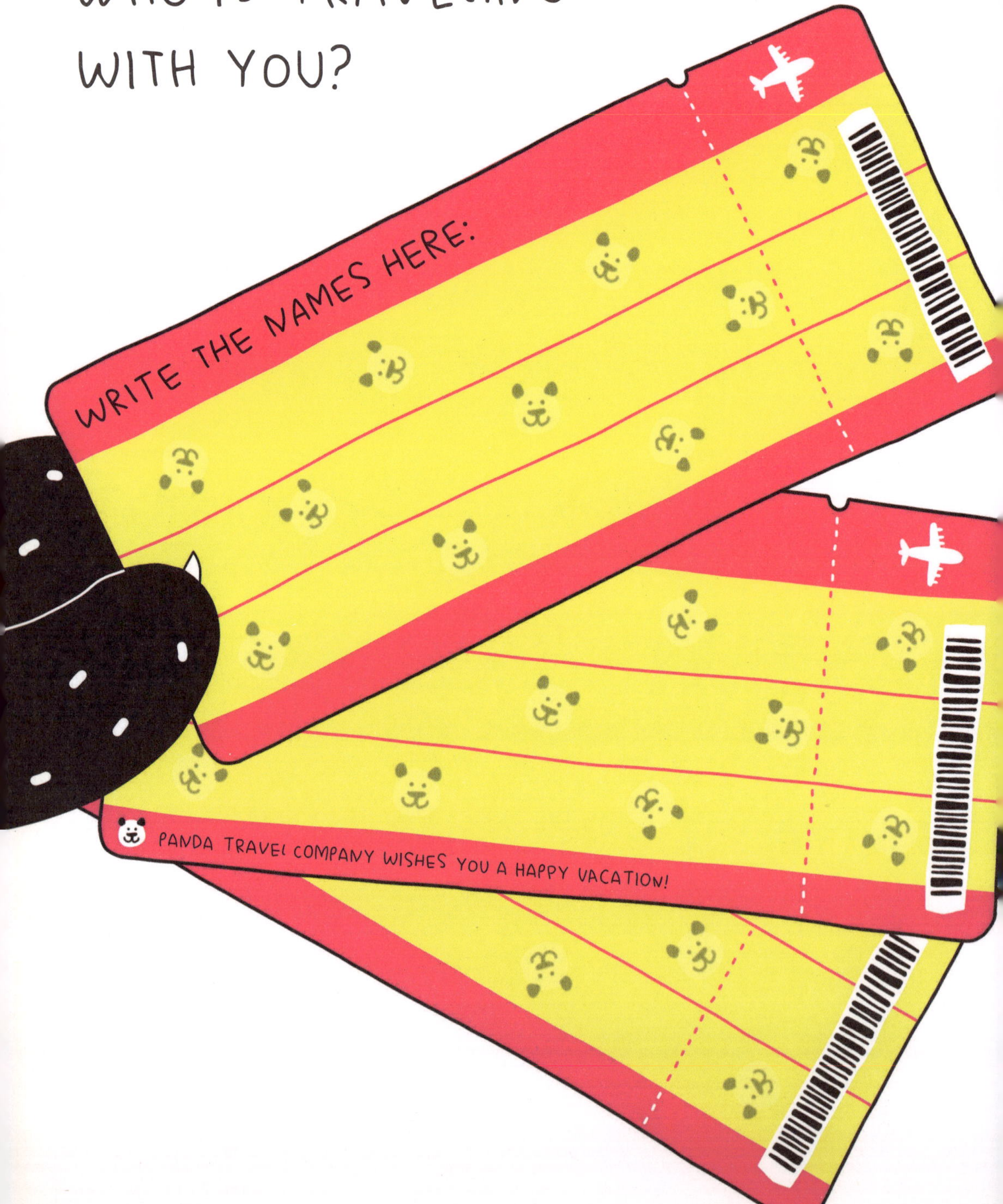

WRITE WHAT YOU ALREADY KNOW

ABOUT THE PLACE YOU ARE GOING TO VISIT.

COLLECT YOUR VACATION
CLOTHES FROM
THE DRY CLEANER.

ENTER THE NUMBERS!

- [ ] (________________________)
- [ ] (________________________)
- [ ] (SEW IN BUTTON)
- [ ] (REMOVE STAIN)
- [ ] (IRON)
- [ ] (FRESHEN UP!!!)

THINGS TO DO BEFORE GOING

WRITE THEM HERE AND MARK THEM WITH AN X WHEN DONE!

CHOOSE THE MUSIC FOR YOUR JOURNEY

- [ ] ROCK
- [ ] POP
- [ ] RAP
- [ ] JAZZ
- [ ] _____

THE SONG THAT YOU MUST TAKE WITH YOU:

IT'S TIME TO SHOW YOUR PASSPORT!

NAME

LAST NAME

DATE OF BIRTH

HEIGHT

COLOR THE LITTLE BOXES

EYES

HAIR

SIGNATURE

DRAW THE STAMPS OF YOUR PREVIOUS TRAVELS

LOGGING IN

DURING YOUR VACATION
YOU CAN COME BACK TO THIS
PART OF THE DIARY
TO LOG SOME SPECIFIC THINGS.

HERE, FOR EXAMPLE, YOU CAN PASTE ALL THE LABELS, TICKETS, AND PAPERS THAT YOU'LL FIND DURING YOUR JOURNEY!

SUPER!
SPF 50
XXL MENU!
LUNCH AND DINNER
GLUE
CITY TOUR
120 MIN.

LIST ALL THE NEW FOODS THAT YOU ARE TRYING ON VACATION.

(YOU CAN DRAW OR WRITE ON THE TABLE!)

MY ABSOLUTE FAVORITE: ______________________

NOT TOO BAD: ________________________________

I GAVE IT A TRY: ____________________________

(NOT FOR ME!!!)

MONITOR THE WEATHER!

DRAW AN X EVERY TIME THAT THE WEATHER CHANGES.

THE MOST BEAUTIFUL
DAY

3 TREASURES THAT YOU HAVE FOUND:

1

2

3

SPECIAL ENCOUNTERS

WRITE DOWN THE MOST INTERESTING PEOPLE
YOU HAVE MET ON YOUR VACATION!

MEETING PLACE:

AGE:

MEETING PLACE:

AGE:

MEETING PLACE:

AGE:

MEETING PLACE:

AGE:

THESE ARE THE BACKS OF THE PREVIOUS PAGE'S FRAMES: ADD THE DETAILS OF YOUR MEETINGS!

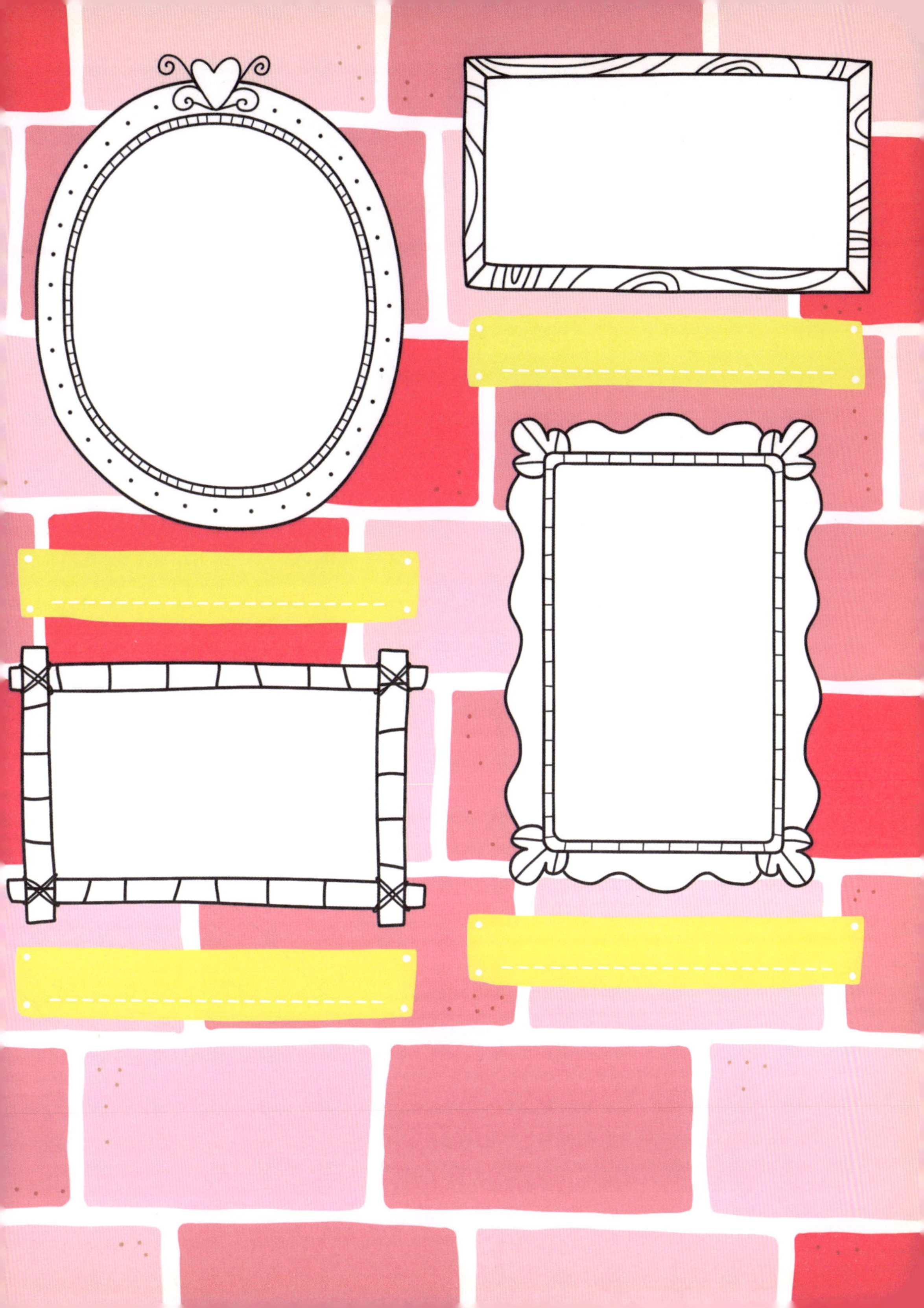

MEETING PLACE:

AGE:

MEETING PLACE:

AGE:

MEETING PLACE:

AGE:

MEETING PLACE:

AGE:

THESE ARE THE BACKS OF THE PREVIOUS PAGE'S FRAMES: ADD THE DETAILS OF YOUR MEETINGS!

DRAW FLAGS,
SIGNS, AND
POSTERS THAT
SPARKED YOUR INTEREST.

ON VACATION!

CHECKING IN.

ARRIVAL TIME:

NUMBER OF GUESTS:

DO YOU HAVE PETS WITH YOU?

TYPE OF ACCOMMODATION:

- [ ] RV
- [ ] TENT
- [ ] BOAT
- [ ] HOTEL
- [ ] HOUSE
- [ ] ____________

HOUSE RULES:

WHAT DO YOU SEE FROM THE WINDOW OF YOUR ACCOMMODATION?

DRAW THE FIRST BREAKFAST OF YOUR VACATION!

WRITE AN
INTERESTING
CONVERSATION THAT YOU HEARD.

THIS IS A YELLOW PAGE!

CLOSE THE DIARY AND ORGANIZE A SUNGLASSES FASHION SHOW.

DATE:

PLACE:

WHO WAS THERE:

HERE IS THE TREASURE HUNT!

CAN YOU FIND THESE THINGS DURING YOUR VACATION? YOU CAN DECIDE THE PRIZE!

A LOST BUTTON

- [ ]

A BLUE ROOF

- [ ]

A DRINK WITH A LITTLE UMBRELLA

- [ ]

- [ ] A PANINI-SHAPED CLOUD

- [ ] A FLOWER TALLER THAN 8 INCHES (20CM)

- [ ] A POODLE

- [ ] AN ANIMAL PAW PRINT

- [ ] A PANDA!

A DAY TO REMEMBER

DATE:

WHO WAS THERE:

ATTACH THE RECEIPT FROM A PLACE WHERE YOU HAD A GREAT MEAL.

****
THANK YOU AND GOODBYE
****

SCORE THE DAY!

THE MOST INTERESTING THING:

THESE ARE BLANK PAGES WHERE YOU CAN WRITE WHATEVER YOU WANT.

N
E
W
S

LET'S EXPLORE!
DISCOVER...
ALTITUDE
AN IMPORTANT MUSUEM
TYPICAL PLANTS
104
TYPICAL
TRANSPORTATION

BEST RESTAURANT
MOST POPULAR GAME
TYPICAL GREETING
A FAMOUS ATTRACTION

DRAW A MIRAGE THAT YOU
THOUGHT YOU SAW ONCE.

MAP OF AN ADVENTURE

DRAW THE ROUTE OF A TRIP YOU MADE.

DESTINATION:

MILES/KM:

DURATION:

GREEN AREA | GAME | WATER AREA | DANGER | FOOD | ------- | -------

DESCRIBE A BIG MEAL YOU HAD!

MENU OF THE DAY

A NICE PLACE
GUIDE

TELL A STORY ABOUT

A PARTICULAR PLACE.

LIST OF THINGS YOU NEED

DATE:

LIST OF ANIMALS YOU'VE SPOTTED

LIST ______________________________

LIST ______________________________

WHAT DOES THE SUNSET LOOK LIKE?

ANOTHER INTERESTING CONVERSATION!

ORGANIZE A NIGHT TRIP.

FIND AT LEAST 3 SOURCES OF STRANGE NOISES.

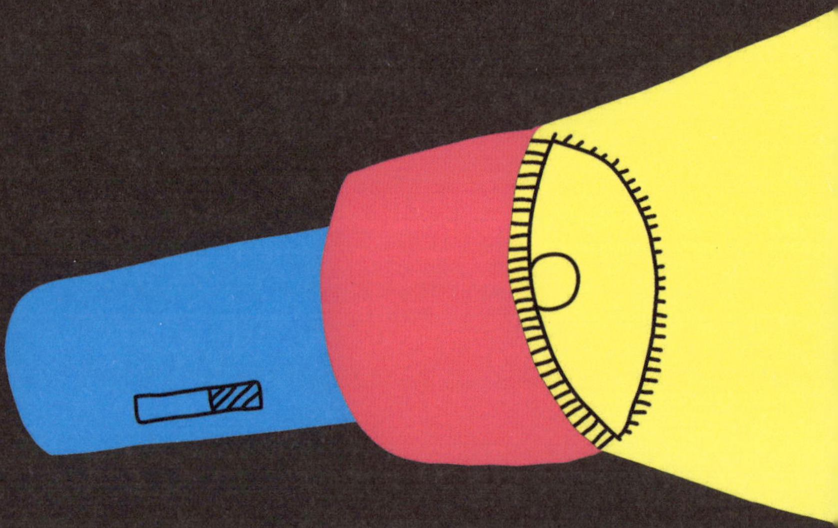

SHARPEN YOUR EYES! CAN YOU SPOT
BEACH
100 YARDS (100M)

HE 13 DIFFERENCES BETWEEN THESE 2 PAGES?
BEACH
200 YARDS (200M)

A DAY TO REMEMBER

DATE:

PICTURE OF THE DAY
(OR A DRAWING!)

WHO WAS THERE:

ATTACH THE RECEIPT FROM A PLACE WHERE YOU HAD A GREAT MEAL.

****
THANK YOU AND GOODBYE
****

SCORE THE DAY

THE MOST INTERESTING THING:

THESE ARE BLANK PAGES WHERE YOU CAN WRITE WHATEVER YOU WANT.

N
E
W
S

MAP OF AN ADVENTURE

DRAW THE ROUTE OF A NICE TRIP YOU MADE.

DESTINATION:

MILES/KM:

DURATION:

GREEN AREA | GAME | WATER AREA | DANGER | FOOD | ------- | -------

THIS PAGE IS BLUE!

CLOSE THE DIARY AND GO TO AN AQUATIC AREA.

DATE:

PLACE:

WHO WAS THERE:

HAVE YOU FOUND ANY MASTERPIECES?

DRAW THE MOST
BEAUTIFUL ONES!

USE LOCAL MATERIALS AND MAKE A WORK OF ART TO GIVE TO THE PLACE THAT HAS WELCOMED YOU.

HERE YOU CAN CREATE A COPY!

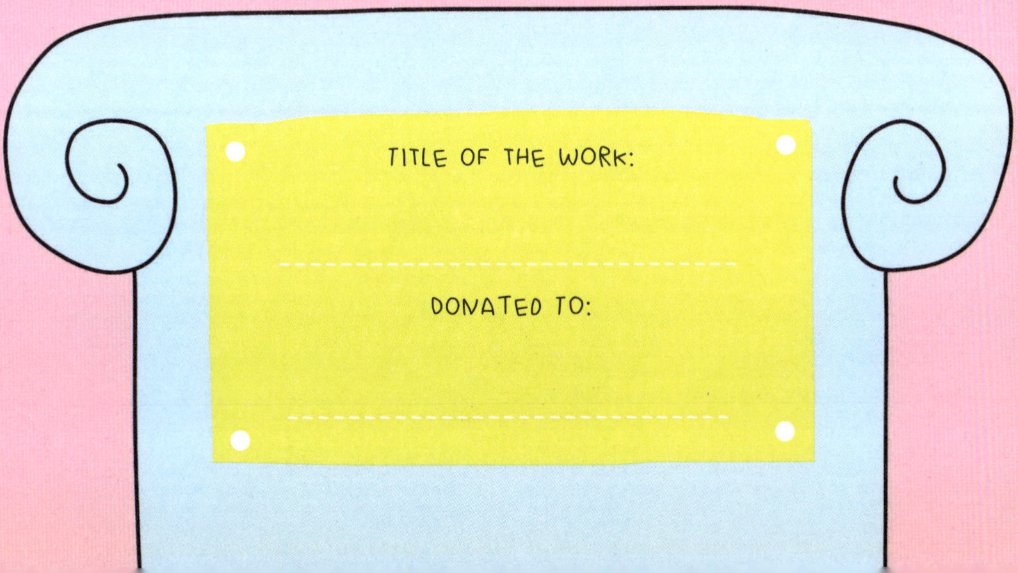

A NICE PLACE
GUIDE

TELL A STORY ABOUT
A PARTICULAR PLACE.

HAVE YOU SPOTTED ANYTHING FAR AWAY?

☐ MAYBE... ☐ NOT YET ☐ YES

DRAW IT INSIDE THE LENSES!

FIND PLAYMATES FOR A MEMORY GAME!

TAKE TURNS OBSERVING THIS PAGE FOR 30 SECONDS AND PLAY BY REMEMBERING ITS DETAILS, WITH QUESTIONS SUCH AS:

HOW MANY STARS ARE THERE?
WHAT COLOR IS THE TOWEL?

LIST OF THINGS YOU NEED

DATE:

LIST OF WORDS YOU LEARNED

LIST OF VERY SPECIAL PLACES

LIST ____________________________

HOW'S THE VIEW AT NIGHT?

REMEMBER THAT THE NIGHT IS YOUNG!

DRAW ALL THE LIGHTS
AND NOCTURNAL SPARKLES
THAT YOU SEE ON YOUR VACATION
(YOU CAN USE LIGHT-COLORED PENCILS,
CHALK, GLOW-IN-THE-DARK STICKERS,
NAIL POLISH...).

A DAY TO REMEMBER

DATE:

WHO WAS THERE:

ATTACH THE RECEIPT FROM A PLACE WHERE YOU HAD A GREAT MEAL.

****
THANK YOU AND GOODBYE
****

SCORE THE DAY

THE MOST INTERESTING THING:

THESE ARE BLANK PAGES WHERE YOU CAN WRITE WHATEVER YOU WANT.

N
E
W
S

DRAW A MIRAGE THAT YOU THOUGHT YOU SAW ONCE.

POSTCARDS

I
3X2!!
WHAT SOUVENIRS HAVE YOU SEEN? DRAW THEM!

COME UP WITH THE POSTER FOR A FILM THAT COULD BE SHOT IN THIS LOCATION.

THIS IS A PINK PAGE!

CLOSE THE DIARY AND DISCOVER

A LOCAL LOVE STORY.

TITLE:

PLACE:

CHARACTERS:

A NICE PLACE
GUIDE

TELL A STORY ABOUT

A PARTICULAR PLACE.

NEVER TRIED BEFORE...

WHAT HAVE YOU DONE FOR THE FIRST TIME DURING THIS VACATION? WRITE OR DRAW!

NEVER TO TRY AGAIN...

WAS THERE SOMETHING DURING YOUR VACATION THAT YOU DON'T WANT TO DO EVER AGAIN?

DESCRIBE
A BIG MEAL YOU HAD!
MENU
OF THE DAY

THIS IS A PAGE IN BLACK AND WHITE!

CLOSE THE DIARY AND ORGANIZE A SHOW OF HAND SHADOWS.

DATE:

PLACE:

WHO WAS THERE:

MAP OF THE JOURNEY HOME

DRAW THE ROUTE BACK HOME.

TYPE OF TRANSPORT:

MILES/KM OF DISTANCE:

ESTIMATED DURATION:

GREEN AREA   GAME   WATER AREA   DANGER   FOOD   -------   -------

GIVE THESE CARDS TO THE FRIENDS
THAT YOU'VE MADE ON VACATION

TO:

TO:

TO:

TO:

HERE ON THE BACK LEAVE THEM A SPECIAL MESSAGE
OR YOUR ADDRESS SO THAT YOU CAN KEEP IN TOUCH!

GIVE THESE CARDS TO THE FRIENDS THAT YOU'VE MADE ON VACATION

TO:

TO:

TO:

TO:

HERE ON THE BACK LEAVE THEM A SPECIAL MESSAGE
OR YOUR ADDRESS SO THAT YOU CAN KEEP IN TOUCH!

THE RETURN
COME BACK SOON!
LET'S GO

HERE YOU ARE ON YOUR WAY BACK HOME! USE THESE LAST PAGES TO RATE YOUR TRIP.

DID YOU TRY BRAIDS ON VACATION?

☐ YES ☐ NO

HAVE YOU COME BACK WITH ANY INJURIES?

☐ YES ☐ NO

HAVE YOU SENT ANY POSTCARDS?

☐ YES ☐ NO

HOW TALL ARE YOU NOW?

_____FEET/CM

DID YOU LEAVE ANYTHING BEHIND ON VACATION?

☐ YES! ☐ NO

DOES YOUR ROOM LOOK THE SAME?

☐ YES ☐ NO...

HAVE YOU BROUGHT SOMETHING SPECIAL
BACK IN YOUR SUITCASE? DRAW IT!

GIVE SOME PRIZES TO YOUR VACATION!

THE STEEPEST CLIMB

THE CRAZY EXCURSION

TRAVELER OF THE YEAR

THE BEST SNACK

IT'S TIME TO SAY GOODBYE, BUT DON'T WORRY: THOSE WHO TRAVEL ONCE, TRAVEL AGAIN.

*

IN THE MEANTIME,
WRITE DOWN THE PLACES THAT
YOU WOULD LIKE TO VISIT NEXT.
(WHEN THE TIME COMES, YOU CAN ALWAYS
START THIS DIARY ALL OVER AGAIN!)

*

PRISCA PRIANO IS THE CREATIVE MIND AND ILLUSTRATOR BEHIND "JOIN THE PANDA!" - A SERIES OF PROJECTS INTENDED TO STIMULATE THE IMAGINATION OF CHILDREN. PRIANO HOLDS A DEGREE IN EDUCATION, AS WELL AS IN YOGA INSTRUCTION. SHE USES THIS DUAL TRAINING TO DEVELOP WORKSHOPS, GAMES, EXCURSIONS, AND YOGA COURSES FOR CHILDREN AT SPECIAL EVENTS, MUSEUMS, AND SCHOOLS.

Piazzale Luigi Cadorna, 6 - 20123 Milan, Italy
www.whitestar.it

Translation: Inga Sempel Pelosi
Editing: Michele Suchomel-Casey

Second printing, January 2024

ISBN 978-88-544-1983-4
2 3 4 5 6   28 27 26 25 24

Printed and manufactured in China
by Guangzhou XY Printing Co.,Ltd, Guang Zhou City

SUPER!
400.
SUPER!
400.